Dear one,
Thanks for Yo
Giving ♡          For
                    you
                         Ps. 46

# SUNRISE IN YOUR SOUL

## By Judith Asmus Hill

PublishAmerica
Baltimore

© 2010 by Judith Asmus Hill
All rights reserved. No part of this book may be reproduced, stored in a retrieval system or transmitted in any form or by any means without the prior written permission of the publishers, except by a reviewer who may quote brief passages in a review to be printed in a newspaper, magazine or journal.

First printing

PublishAmerica has allowed this work to remain exactly as the author intended, verbatim, without editorial input.

Hardcover 978-1-4512-7134-8
Softcover 978-1-4512-7133-1
PUBLISHED BY PUBLISHAMERICA, LLLP
www.publishamerica.com
Baltimore

Printed in the United States of America

# DEDICATION

I dedicate this work of poetry and passages from the Bible, to all who are in need of Jesus love, encouragement and forgiveness, which is SUNRISE IN YOUR SOUL. To all of you who have given or will ever give His sunshine to others souls, I dedicate these poems.


Sending you God's kind of love,

Judy

# ACKNOWLEDGMENTS

I would like to praise and thank my Heavenly Father, who sent Jesus Christ to die on the cross for my sins and the sins or all mankind! He brought SUNRISE IN MY SOUL!

I would also like to thank my sweet, precious husband, Jim, for his help and support so that I could complete "SUNRISE IN YOUR SOUL."

A big thank you goes to my wonderful children and grandchildren and my awesome sisters and friends who have encouraged me to continue to write poetry to bring God's SON shine to our souls!

# Table of Contents

## POEMS & PASSAGES
### That Will
## GIVE YOU GUIDANCE

## POEMS & PASSAGES
### To Help Find
## REAL SUCCESS

# POEMS & PASSAGES
# TO BRING
# SUNRISE IN YOUR SOUL

For the Lord God is a sun and shield; the Lord will give grace and glory; no good thing will He withhold from those who walk uprightly.

PSALM 84:11

Weeping may endure for a night, but joy cometh in the morning.

PSALM 30:5A

# THE SUNRISE ON THE OCEAN

It's so incredible to the human eye, to see the sun rise in the sky.

It rises slowly, as to extol, as the ocean waves swiftly roll.

God is a big and mighty God, He springs the flowers from the sod.

Why would I doubt that He answers prayer, when I see He gives such loving care.

Every detail of my life, He surely plans it out, Lord forgive me for the times that I succumb to doubt.


And immediately, Jesus stretched out His hand and caught him, and said to him, "O you of little faith, why did you doubt?"

And when they got into the boat, the wind ceased.

MATTHEW 14:31 & 32

Through the Lord's mercies we are not consumed, because His compassions fail not, they are new every morning: Great is Thy faithfulness. The Lord is my portion, says my soul, therefore I hope in Him.

LAMENTATIONS 3:23 & 24

# FOOT PRINTS IN THE SAND

Early in the morning, up to see the sun
Sparkling on the water, my day has just begun.

No storm in sight, the birds sing their sweet song
Today is good, but others very long.

At any given moment, blue skies can turn to gray
You think you're going under, what can help me stay.

Jesus said He'd carry me, when trials come so fast
Like footprints in the sand, He carries me at last.

I'll never be forsaken, the Bible tells me so
His Word will be my mainstay that for sure I know.


When thou passest through the water, I will be with thee:
and through the rivers, they shall not overflow thee:
when thou walkest through the fire, thou shalt not be burned;
neither shall the flame kindle upon thee.

ISAIAH 43:2

# TREE BLOSSOMS

As the tree blossoms danced in the wind today
My heart looked up and began to pray...

Lord help my heart to trust in You
And always believe in what You do.

Even though I don't understand...
You'll surely be there with Your loving hand.


But the Lord who is faithful, who shall stablish you,
And keep you from evil.

II THESSALONIANS 3:3

# THE PALM TREE

When God made the Palm Tree He did it with such grace
To look at it inspires me; its leaves are like green lace.

It bends and waves in costal storms
But when at peace, my soul it warms.

When storms come bursting in our hearts
It bends and waves our inward parts.

Our soul, spirit, body must be planted in God's way
Then the devil will not bend us, we will not go astray.

We must decide to follow God each and every day
Obeying God's Holy Word will surely win the fray.


The righteous shall flourish like a palm tree:
he shall grow like a cedar in Lebanon.

PSALM 92:12

This is my comfort in my affliction, for
Your Word has given me life.

PSALM 119:50

# PREPARE FOR THE STORMS

It's a beautiful day with sunshine and breeze
Not a cloud in the sky, you feel at ease.

Someone else is guiding the boat
Don't have to worry, it's easy afloat.

Then out of no where in blows a storm
You're out of control, it's not the norm.

What do you do when control is not yours
Do you trust in the Lord that He'll calm the roars.

Are you always too busy with life to take time
We must place God first with out reason or rhyme.

Prepare for the storms every day that you live
Then you'll be ready, have plenty to give.


The Lord is good, a strong hold in the day of trouble;
and He knoweth them that trust in Him.

NAHUM 1:7


Who comforteth us in all our tribulation, that we may be able to comfort
them which are in any trouble, by the comfort wherewith we ourselves
are comforted of God.

II CORINTHIANS 1:4

# TRUST HIS HEART

When you can't see God's hand…
Trust His Heart

He'll make a way…
Do His part

His Word will help
Take time to read…

In His Word…
You will succeed.


Every Word of God is pure: He is a shield unto
them that put their trust in Him.

PROVERBS 30:5

# LOOK FOR THAT FLOWER

Take time to smell a rose
Before it's petals close.
The scent will only
Last a while…
Before it's thrown
Into a pile.

Enjoy the simply things
In life…
Laughter, hugs,
Give up the strife
Many lives are
In a mess…
Because they didn't
Deal with stress.

The joy of Jesus gives us peace
Give Him your cares
Let anger cease.
Go out tomorrow…
Look for that flower
Then let God be your mighty tower.


The joy of the Lord is your strength.

Nehemiah 8:10

# JUST A STONE

Remember when Goliath fell
You say, "With just a stone?"
David knew it was God's power
Coming from His throne.

David had to take that step
And believe the giant would fall.
The only way Goliath fell
Was on God's name to call.

When we have giants in our lives
We'll always understand.
The only way to win is by
Taking our Lord's hand.

It's in His mighty hand
The answer's truly there.
God speaks through His word
Our burdens He will bear.

When you think about that stone
And where your problems are...
Know the answer's only Jesus,
That Bright Morning Star.

Then said David to the Philistine, Thou comest
to me with a sword, and with a spear, and with a
shield: but I come to thee in the name of the Lord
of hosts, the God of the armies of Israel, whom
thou hast defied.

I SAMUEL 17:45

# MY FAVORITE TREE

My favorite tree is the Evergreen Tree
Its branches so stately and free.
It reminds me of Jesus, my best friend
Because it's needles remain to the end.

Jesus suffered and died for us all
All can be saved if on His name they call.
The Evergreen Tree stands tall in the heat
Sustains in the snow and even the sleet.

When hard times come as they surely will
Read His Word and then be still.
If we stay close to Jesus and cling to the cross
Our lives will not experience loss.


Jesus Christ the same yesterday today
and forever.

HEBREWS 13:8

# HEARTSTRINGS

The strings of my heart are very fragile
I pray everyday that hurts will be gradual.
When a string is too tight, it will surely break
Prayer alters that process for Jesus sake.

When I gave my heart to Jesus many years ago
He promised to be with me, and I'd always know…
I'd know to trust my God as the keeper of my heart
If I stayed close to Him, It wouldn't break apart.

When my heartstrings had been so sorely tried
The tears came, I cried and cried.
God's Holy Spirit was there for me
Taking my burden to set my heart free.

Don't be afraid to give Jesus your heart
He will always be there to do His part.
Weeping may endure for a night
But joy comes with the morning light.

The Spirit of the Lord is upon me, because he hath
anointed me to preach the gospel to the poor; he hath
sent me to heal the broken-hearted, to preach
deliverance to the captives, and recovering of sight
to the blind, to set at liberty them that are bruised.

LUKE 4:18

Weeping may endure for a night, but joy cometh in the
Morning.

PSALM 30:5b

# A BLUE SKY

Every morning out the window I look
After reading the Bible, my favorite book.
I look out to see what the day will bring…
Hoping clouds carry my favorite thing.

Then I turn my thoughts to a better way
No matter what happens, during this day.
God stays by my side in good times and bad
He'll show His grace if I'm happy or sad.

When you see a blue sky, that might turn to gray
Don't worry about that throughout your day.
He knows how to make every thing right
God's grace will be there from morning 'til night.


My grace is sufficient for thee: for
My strength is made perfect in weakness.

II CORINTHIANS 12:9

# SPRINGTIME

I love to see the Red Buds
And the Dogwoods blooming there…
And the Robin perching in the trees
With its song to share.

We all like that precious time
When everything is new.
We're thankful when a storm has passed
So many things to do.

I want to wait upon you Lord
When testings come my way.
In Your Word is Springtime
That's surely here to stay.


Wait on the Lord: be of good courage, and He shall
strengthen thine heart: wait, I say on the Lord.

PSALM 27:14

# GOD'S ANGELS

Where do angels come from
They're sent from Heaven above
God sends them down to help us
It shows of His great love.

They must be very busy
Each one has their task
When we are in need
All we have to do is ask.

We ask according to His word
They're always on His call.
Some are there for worship
Or to keep us from a fall.

His ministering spirits
Are always around.
We'll be forever grateful
As their help we've found.


The angel of the Lord encamps
round about them that fear Him,
and delivereth them.

PSALM 34:7

# MAKING MELODY IN YOUR HEART

A song is very sweet
It gives you dancing feet.
When you're lonely or sad
It will make your heart glad.

You can lift your praise
Your spirit it will raise.
The angels come to join you
They love to praise God, too.

Worship with all of your heart
When you're sad, it's a good place to start.
We all have things to overcome
But the Lord will help us, and then some.

David played his harp for Saul…
Depression left, enjoyed by all.
The Lord rejoices over us with singing
Give back a melody, keep the rafters ringing.


Speaking to yourselves in psalms and hymns and
spiritual songs, singing and making melody in your
heart to the Lord.


EPHESIANS 5:19

# POEMS & PASSAGES
## That Will Help You
# LOVE FAMILY & FRIENDS

My little children, let us not love in word or in tongue, but in deed and in truth.

And this is His commandment; that we should believe on the name of His son Jesus Christ and love one another, as He gave us commandment.

I John 4: 18 & 23

# A MOTHER'S PRAYER

I pray for wisdom for being a mother
This role in life is like no other.
Much of my role is joy delayed...
Until then, I won't be afraid.

Lord help me be willing to give of myself
Put my book down, take theirs off the shelf.
Rocking the cradle at the midnight hour
Give me more strength and also your power.

Help me not mind when I can't buy the best
More for the children, in this I rest.
May the things that I do match the things that I say
Pour your love through me, truly, I pray.

There's been many tears
Over life's broad years...
Tears of joy and tears of sorrow
Trusting You Lord, for each tomorrow.

My prayer is that they'll always stay
Close by Your side and never stray.
I cannot ask for a life without trials
With Your strength, they'll come out with smiles.


And the very God of peace sanctify you
wholly; and I pray God, your whole spirit
and soul and body be preserved blameless
unto the coming of our Lord Jesus Christ.

I THESSALONIANS 5:23

29

# PRAYER FOR FATHERS

I ask, dear Lord, You bless each dad
With Your love upon their face.
Giving to their families
All of Your amazing grace.

Help kids forgive their fathers
When they don't do it right.
Let there be no bitterness
No burning in their sight.

When they see their fathers
Let them see with eyes of love.
Knowing 'cause of Jesus
There's forgiveness from above.

Let father's not provoke their kids
Be loving and yet firm.
When Your love speaks through them
It'll make the devil squirm.

To a child time means love
So give your time away...
If you don't give them time,
They surely might fall prey.

Help dads to pray a blessing
With a lot of details there.
It will truly change their lives
And let them know You care.

And ye fathers, provoke not your children
to wrath: but bring them up in the nurture and
admonition of the Lord.

EPHESIANS 6:4

# MIRACLE OF BIRTH

There's nothing like a newborn
To set your heart on fire
The miracle of birth…
Is surely to inspire.

A baby sent from heaven above
Sparks within your heart, God's love
Tiny fingers are a joy…
Caring not, if girl or boy.

The miracle of birth
Best part of God's creation
It's truly so amazing
Beyond imagination.


And God said, Let us make
man in our image, after our
likeness;

GENESIS 1:26a

# MY GRANDPA'S HANDS

My Grandpa's hands were really rough
He worked so hard, he was very tough.
He would take those hands and grab for mine
Younger sisters and brothers would wait in line.

When grandma died, how lonely was he
My grandpa's hands wiped tears, you see.
He'd come to the farm to help my dad
Working with his hands made his heart glad.

Many meals we ate on the farm
My grandpa's hands prayed for no harm.
He prayed for us seven to see God's love
It brought the angels down from above.

My grandpa's hands are resting now
My three son's hands now wipe their brow.
Their hands are busy serving the Lord
Leaving a legacy of a three-fold chord.


And let the beauty of the Lord our God
be upon us: and establish thou the work of
our hands upon us; yea the work of our hands
establish thou it.

PSALM 90:17

# WAVING At THE WINDOW

After we were married, this tradition always tarried…
Every time back home we came, it would always be the same
As we left, my parents at the window they would be
The waving of their hands so we could clearly see.

It warmed our hearts and meant so much to me…
I don't think I ever told them how it really set me free.
We truly knew they loved us very much
To take the time to have that special touch.

As our family grew little hands were waving, too…
When my father died, my mom alone waved through.
My mother has gone home; it's our turn to do that now
To carry on that love, 'til at death's door we bow.

Our grandkids now look forward to see us as we wave…
I now wave alone since we've laid grandpa in the grave.
Grandpa now is waving in the presence of the Lord
Take time for good traditions, do all you can afford.

The Lord has brought another man so kind and true…
To be my precious husband, our lives in tune with YOU.
Now we wave at the window as our family departs
Hoping that they feel our love deep within their hearts!


If there be therefore any consolation in Christ, if
any fellowship of the Spirit, if any bowels and mercies,
fulfill ye my joy, that ye be like-minded, having the same
love, being of one accord, of one mind.

PHILIPIANS 2:1, 2

# THE TABLE

I think about my childhood
What memories surface most…
It's the times around the table
Where my parents were the hosts.

Sharing things that happened
During school or at play…
It's a time that I looked
Forward to each and every day.

Around our table prayer took place
It brought a smile on each face…
Around our table the Bible was read
After we talked and our face was fed.

Be sure your table is at the center of your life
Words shared there can dispel much strife.
The table helps join in one accord
It will make sweet memories shared by the Lord.


Thy wife shall be as a fruitful vine by the
sides of thine house: thy children like olive plants
round about thy table.

PSALM 128:3

# THE OLD SCHOOL HOUSE

The one room school is a thing of the past
Its walls hold memories that will last and last.
The teacher then, had a big job to do...
They trusted God to help them through.

Molding and shaping a child's mind
Is a greater work to help mankind.
Teaching them more than what's in a book
To see beyond, each time that they look.

To see a hope and a plan for their life
Sometimes it's their teacher that helps in the strife.
Many homes represented there...
Some have parents that don't really care.

A teacher can help fill the gap for them
A stitch of love can hold up their hem...
A hem that is tattered and totally torn
A teacher can show them a life that's reborn.


This is my commandment that ye love
one another, as I have loved you.

JOHN 15:12

For the law of the Spirit of life in Christ Jesus hath
made me free from the law of sin and death.

ROMANS 8:2

# FRIENDS

A friend is one
Who makes you smile
Even in the midst
Of trial.

She's there to help
When times are rough.
Her caring ways
Are always enough.

Whatever you ask
She'll try to do…
Her love has been
Tested, tried and true.

She gives advice
That passes the test…
It's from the Word
It is the best.

I want to make time
To be with her…
Life passes too quickly
That's for sure.


A friend loveth at all times.

PROVERBS 17:17

# TIME FOR TEA

On lonely days when your heart is sad
Take time for tea, life won't seem so bad.
Call up a friend and share your heart
God loves through friends, that is His part.

The gift of listening is quite an art
It brings much healing to your heart.
Many will just not take the time
They have no vision, no reason or rhyme.

They want to have their own selfish way
Too busy to give the time of day.
If someone listens with caring love
Problems may be solved by the Father above.

So get out your prettiest china cup
Take the time to lift others up.
When to God your day you give
He'll plan it out for others to live.


Bear ye one another's burdens, and so
fulfill the law of Christ.
As we have therefore opportunity, let us
do good unto all men, especially unto them
who are of the household of faith.

GALATIANS 6:2, 10

# THE WALL

Sometimes you want to reach out
To others; be a friend.
There seems to be a wall
It's really a dead end.

You try to talk again
But the feeling is still there…
You ask the Lord about it
As you bow your head in prayer.

It seems the Lord was telling me
As I talked to Him one day…
He said your friend is filled with fear
She's built a wall to help her stay.

It helps her feel protected
As she stays within the wall.
The Lord said keep on loving her
And pray the wall will fall.

I know that love and prayer
Are a mighty combination…
I will also read God's word
For enlightened revelation.


And to love Him with all the heart, and with all the
understanding, and with all the soul, and with all the
strength, and to love his neighbor as himself, is more
than all whole burnt offerings and sacrifices.

MARK 12:33

The Lord is my light and my salvation; who shall I fear?
The Lord is the strength of my life; of whom shall I be afraid?

PSALM 27:1

# A CARDBOARD BOX

A cardboard box
Has many uses…
It holds priceless crystal
Or vegetable juices.

If you look at the outside
They all look the same…
But when you see on the inside
They all have a name.

We can't be too busy
We must show our care…
Take time to listen
See what's inside there.

To hear a teenager
Share their heart
Just to listen
Would be your part.

You'll heal your spouse
When they're down and out
Take time to listen—
It keeps them from doubt.

Next time you see
A cardboard box
Remember it's listening
That opens the locks.

And now abideth faith, hope and love,
these three, but the greatest of these is love.

1 CORINTHIANS 13:13

Judy and her older sister, Joyce, who went to heaven early at 37
years old. How about that cool car in the background!

Psalm 98:5

"Send A Song"

Judy M. Asmus
Singer with Autoharp
(for any occasion)

Liberty Hi Rd.
Haskins, Oh 43525
Ph. (419) 823-1717

Judy's first ministry photo in early 1980's and her first ministry card.

Judy at WJYM Radio where the "SEND A SONG" program was aired live for 7 ½ years. It was also aired in Israel through "VOICE OF HOPE," and in Africa, through "FAR EAST BROADCASTING," for 2 years.

The Michigan/Ohio Choir(CMI) was the first Gospel Choir to ever sing in the Kremlin. On this very stage in Russia, Judy & Dean(1st husband) handed out Russian New Testaments to Government Leaders, only a few days after the collapse of the Soviet Union in 1991. They sang in this choir for 17 years.

As the sun is setting on the Mediterranean Sea, Judy is singing a song called, "One Less Stone." This song was accompanied by the Michigan/Ohio Gospel Choir (CMI).

This is a picture of the CMI Gospel Choir where Judy and Dean, were singing on the walls of the Citadel of David in Jerusalem. We took part in the Jerusalem 3000 mission event.

Judy with Jamey Schmitz, President and CEO of our local Christian TV Station WLMB, in Toledo, OH, where she has been hosting the Telethons for 11 years.

This is the cover for THE ASMUS F AMIL Y SINGER'S first recording, "AN OPEN DOOR."

"LABOR OF LOVE," the CD cover to "THE ASMUS FAMILY SINGER'S second recording.

One of Judy's first solo albums, where she recorded some of her own original songs called, "LIGHT A FIRE WITH MUSIC."

"SEASONS OF HARVEST," was the cover for. "THE ASMUS FAMILY SINGER'S 3rd album.

JUDY ASMUS

"Willows By The Waters"

"WILLIOWS BY THE WATER," is the cover for one of Judy's first solo albums.

*"Send A Song At Christmastime"*

This is the cover for Judy's Christmas CD, 'SEND A SONG AT CHRISTMASTIME," which also includes some of her original songs.

Judy with her daughter, Beth Motsinger and her 5 granddaughters, Madeline, Mckinley, Katelyn, Stephanie & Noelle, singing at the Wo. Co. Fair in Bowling Green, OH.

Judy with her new husband of 2 ½ years. They married 2/29/08, after their mates went to heaven in 2006. They thank the Lord every day for bringing them together! Jim teaches the Word and Judy sings the Word at jails, nursing homes, retreats, church services & Christian gatherings of all kinds!

# THE BASKET

A basket carries many a thing
A score of music that helps us sing.
It can carry food to a lonely neighbor
Filled with goodies, the love of our labor.

Once in a while our basket is set
In a corner, no need can be met…
For we are the ones in need of care
In come the baskets, their love to share.

We also reap whatever we sow
So take time now to bend the bow,
You never know when your time will come
The arrow goes forth with a special hum.

So fill your basket with love while you can
Fill it with flowers, or cake in a pan…
Take care of others with God's love
He'll send baskets from above.


And let us not be weary in well doing:
for in due season we shall reap, if we faint not.

GALATIANS 6:9

# NO PLACE LIKE HOME

You may drive through the mountains
See the snow-capped scenery there,
Or feel the waves along the beach...
As the sun shines on your hair,

You may go to hear the music
In the hills of Tennessee,
Or bask in the sunset...
In the warmth of Waikiki,

But there's nothing like the feeling
To see the cattle roam,
In the flatland of Ohio...
There's just no place like home,

A memory of my childhood
That I remember most,
Was the crowing of the rooster...
And the smell of home baked toast,

The sound that set my ears on edge
Was the filing of the hoes,
When my father called us early
To weed those old corn rows,

Every Sunday morning
I would sing with all my heart,
In our little country church...
All our family was a part,

Getting ready for our hometown fair
Our club steers we would comb,

Living in Wood County...
There's just no place like home.


When I remember these things, I pour out my
soul within me. For I used to go with the
multitude; I went with them to the house of
God, with the voice of joy and praise.

PSALM 42:4

# POEMS & PASSAGES
## That Will
# GIVE YOU GUIDANCE

For I know the thoughts that I think toward
you, saith the Lord, thoughts of peace, and
not of evil, to give you and expected end.

Then shall you call upon Me, and you shall go and pray unto Me, and
I will hearken unto you.

And you shall seek Me, and find Me, when you shall search for Me with
all your heart.

Jeremiah 29:11-13

# PRAYER FOR GUIDANCE

Lord, I really need to hear Your word
Your advice is the best I've ever heard…
So many voices come to me
They try so hard to help me see.

Your Rhema word is what I need
I take my time Your voice to heed.
The answer I'm seeking is found in You…
Others can help me; yes that is true.

When You open a door, I want to go through
I just want to make sure that it is from You.
I wait for the peace in my spirit as well
Then I'll go forth with joy Your story to tell.


I will instruct thee and teach thee in the
way which thou shalt go: I will guide thee with
mine eye.

PSALM 32:8




## INCLINE YOUR EAR

God's creation is beautiful
The sky very blue…

His sunshine warms your face
When you stand in its hue.

There's never a dull moment
When you are outside.
Walk and see along the beach
At evening tide.

God uses His creation
To tell us things.
If we have an ear to hear
Heaven and nature sings.

God spoke through Balaam's donkey
For Gideon, dew on fleece.
If you have an ear to hear
He'll surely speak His piece.

For Moses, it was a burning bush
For Noah it was a dove.
God uses His creation
To give us signs of love.

Be sure to have an ear to hear
What the Spirit says to you…
He may guide you
With a dew-filled fleece
Or give you peace through
Clouds of blue.


Incline your ear, and come unto me;
hear, and your soul shall live.

ISAIAH 55:3

# GIVING IS A WAY OF LIFE

When your heart's entwined
With Jesus heart…
Giving to His kingdom
Is a very large part,

It's a very large part
Of everything you do.
If you are unselfish
You'll always make it through.

When you give of your time
Talents and treasure…
Joy is released that
Only heaven can measure.

Whatever seeds you sow
For the Lord…
He always gives plenty
For your reward.


Give, and it shall be given unto you;
good measure, pressed down, and shaken
together, and running over, shall men give
into your bosom, For with the same measure
that ye mete withal it shall be measured to
you again.

LUKE 6:38

# WALK IN THE SPIRIT

There are days when your jaw is set
Fired up, your match you've met…
You've met your flesh and you must deal
Before it becomes much more real.

Down on your knees, you fall
On the Lord's name you call.
He's there the instant you ask
He'll help with this unending task.

It's always good to know
That by His strength we go.
We don't have to go it alone…
He's waiting to help as we seek His throne.


Therefore, brethren, we are debtors not
to the flesh, to live after the flesh. For if ye
live after the flesh, ye shall die: but if ye
through the Spirit, do mortify the deeds of the
body, ye shall live.

ROMANS 8:12, 13

# A HAPPY DAY

When you wake up with morning light
God's sun is truly a lovely sight.
Know that it's a happy day
Because His love is here to stay.

There's nothing else that you can do
To make God's love more tried and true.
Some days you wake with heavy heart
It's very hard to make your start.

Before your feet touch the floor
Take time with God; good things in store
He'll help you overcome the fear...
Start your day by drawing near.

Draw nigh to God and He will draw
nigh to you.

JAMES 4:8

# GOD'S SUNSET

One of the nicest times of my day
I look out the window to see the sun's ray
Sometimes it's pink, or has soft golden hue...
Then not long after comes the fresh fallen dew.

My thoughts turn to God at the setting of sun
I want to make sure all my work has been done.
My work that He's chosen for that day...
Each moment is precious, I must not delay.


I must work the works of Him that sent me,
While it is day; the night cometh, when no
man can work.

JOHN 9:4

# WARMED BY THE BRANCH

Fall is coming
Summer soon to close…
Flowers will fade
You'll not find a rose.

But once in a while
Tucked under a branch
You'll find a rose
Just by happen stance.

Then you'll know
His power was there…
Protecting the flower
To show of His care.

The frost couldn't touch it
Hidden away.
The branch warmed it
Day by day,

The Holy Spirit
Is like that, you know
If you pray in the Spirit
You'll surely glow.

The glow will be warming
To many others
You will find His Spirit
To help sisters and brothers.

In whom ye also are builded together
for an habitation of God through the Spirit.

EPHESIANS 2:22

# THE BLADE OF GRASS

A blade of grass makes a meadow green
One tiny blade grouped with many unseen.
In order to look good each blade must be cut
It's the same for us, or we get in a rut.

It's quite a shock when the herbicides flow
Though in the end, it's good for the show.
God has a plan to make us grow...
Sometimes it's shocking but yet He will know.

He'll know when to weed and when to trim
It may bring tears, full to the brim...
But the end result is what He sees
And we must be patient like the ants and the bees.

So if you want to be part of a beautiful lawn
You must believe that the night precedes dawn.
If you are called to be the President's green...
Be prepared for more trimming and work to be seen.

The grass is always greener across the fence
That's a lie from Satan, don't be dense.
Go forth my beloved, says the Lord to each one
You're part of His body; the victory's been won.


Verily, verily, I say, unless a corn of wheat
fall into the ground and die, it abideth alone:
but if it die, it bringeth forth much fruit.

JOHN 12:24

# THE TOP OF THE TREE

When we were young and healthy
It was fun to climb a tree.
Some were not content
On the lower branch to be.

Some climbed to the top
And looked out just to see
How far they could reach
For fruit; that was the key,

The key to our salvation
Is a gift from God that's free.
It was truly paid by Jesus
When He hung upon that tree.

Reach out accept God's love
And share it with your brother.
He will surely bless your life
Remove sin like no other.


For the Son of man is come to seek
and to save that which was lost.

LUKE 19:10

Who Himself bore our sins in His own
body on the tree, that we, having died to sins,
might live for righteousness…by whose
Stripes you were healed.

1 PETER 2:24

# FORGET YOURSELF

When the day is filled with gloom
Give our Jesus lot's of room.

Room for Him to truly speak
Even when you're feeling weak.

Let Him show you how to live
Ask what you can do to give.

If you give it helps your heart
Forget yourself & do your part.


Give and it shall be given unto you;
good measure,Pressed down, and shaken
together, and running over, shall men give
into your bosom. For with the same measure
that ye mete withal it shall be measured to you again.

LUKE 6:38

# SHOW ME HOW TO LIVE

When things get hectic and life seems tough
You begin to worry; think God's not big enough.

Not big enough to heal your heart
One that is broken completely apart.

Not big enough to find you a mate
Or give you a job with a better rate.

Not big enough your body to heal
Or give you that contract business deal.

Then you repent and ask God to forgive
Please Lord, show me how to live.

I know that I can find out if I read your Word,
If I don't take the time, advice will not be heard.


But they that wait upon the Lord shall renew their
strength; they shall mount up with wings as eagles;
they shall run, and not be weary; and they shall
walk, and not faint.

ISAIAH 40:31

# CONTENTMENT

Why do we murmur, why do we complain
Hardly ever satisfied, never like the rain.

We're just like the Israelites, always wanting more
Why don't we trust our God for what He has in store.

Father please forgive us, help us to be content
Help us trust Your Word before our time is spent.

In Your presence there's always pleasure…
So let God's Word be your greatest treasure.


You will show me the path of life; in Your presence is
fullness of joy; at Your right hand are pleasures forevermore.

PSALM 16:11

Not that I speak in regard to need, for I have learned in
whatever state I am, to be content.

PHILIPPIANS 4:11

# SOWING AND REAPING

When I was but a little girl, I remember mama's garden
I loved to smell the flowers, but time for hoeing; asked for pardon.

I soon began to notice if I planted just one seed
My harvest wasn't plentiful, left me with a need.

As I grew up, I asked the Lord to come into my heart
Then I planted many seeds, for others brand new start.

Do not be deceived, my friend, the Bible is our guide
If you sow much in the kingdom, a great harvest is supplied.


Do not be deceived, God is not mocked; for whatever a man sows,
that he will he also reap.
For he who sows to his flesh, will of the flesh reap corruption,
but he who sows to the Spirit, will of the Spirit reap everlasting life.

GALATIANS 6:7, 8

# THE STIRRING

There's a stirring in your heart
It seems you've lost your peace.
You try to pass it off
And wish that it would cease.

It's there when you awake
Or when you try to sleep.
You tell your friends about it
And hope that they will keep.

Keep the stirring of your heart
That no one else may know.
When you don't know what's wrong with you
Please don't let it show.

Then you take special time
And set before God's throne.
In His word, He speaks to you
And tells you of His own.

He tells you His own story
About the stirring of your heart...
There's something you're to do for Him
It surely is your part.

Be still and know that I am God
He truly says to you.
Stir up the gift and use it
His peace will come anew.

Wherefore I put thee in remembrance that
thou stir up the gift of God, which is in thee by
the putting on of my hands.
For God hath not given us the spirit of fear;
but of power, and of love, and a sound mind

.

II TIMOTHY 1:6, 7

# POEMS & PASSAGES
## To Help Find
## REAL SUCCESS

The Book of the Law shall not depart out
Of your mouth, but you shall meditate in it day and night, that you may
observe to do
According to all that is written in it. For
Then you will make your way prosperous, and then you will have good
success.

Have I not commanded you? Be strong and of good courage; do not be
afraid, nor be dismayed, for the Lord your God is with you wherever
you go.

Joshua 1:8, 9

# UNDER HIS COVERING

There's nothing so great as
To be in the gate…
Protected because of your love
And not hate.

Your love for God's laws
Will keep you protected.
There's comfort in knowing
You won't be rejected.

You're under God's covering
When you obey.
Whenever we sin
Repentance must stay.

You're on your own
When you're out of His covering.
Make sure you obey
His angels are hovering.


For the eyes of the Lord are over the
Righteous, and His ears are open unto their
prayers: but the face of the Lord is against
them that do evil.
And who is he that will harm you, if ye be
followers of that which is good?

I PETER 3:12, 13

# REMOVE THE DIRT

It's time to clean house
Said the Lord to me.
In the natural…
I surely can see.

There's food spots and webs
Dust here and there.
I wanted to clean…
But no time to spare.

Bigger things had
Called my name.
I wanted to do them…
My mind was lame.

Isn't it like that
At times in our life.
We want to change…
But we give in to strife,

Only Jesus removes
Spiritual stains
His blood on the cross…
Forgiveness remains.


Looking unto Jesus the author and finisher
of our faith; who for the joy that was set before
Him endured the cross, despising the shame, and is
set down at the right hand of the throne of God.

HEBREWS 12:2

# THE FUNNEL

Why do we want a funnel
When pouring alone might do
It will keep us from spilling...
And it's time saving, too.

There are times in our lives
When God will use the funnel.
He must pour in swiftly...
May feel dark, like a tunnel.

It's at those times of funneling
We can grow so quickly.
Don't be too surprised...
If He pours when you are sickly.


No chastening for the present seemeth
to be joyous, but grievous: nevertheless
afterward it yieldeth the peaceable fruit of
righteousness unto them which are exercised
thereby.

HEBREWS 12:11

# THE TRUMPET SOUNDS

Someday you'll hear that certain sound
In your spirit spinning round and round.
The trumpet will sound with a stunning note—-
It truly will bring a lump in your throat.

Only those who cultivate a listening ear
Those who have taken the time to hear.
Will know that sound within their heart
Many will miss it; they won't do their part.

They'll be too busy with the pleasures of life
Running to and fro in the midst of strife.
They won't scale down to what really matters
Hearing only sounds of selfish clatters.

What will it take to break the chains
So that only God's voice still remains—-
It will take a decision to obey His word
Then the sounding of His trumpet will be heard.


Blow the trumpet in Zion, and sound an alarm
in my holy mountain: let all the inhabitants of the
land tremble: for the day of the Lord is at hand.

JOEL 2:1

# A NEW YEAR

The end of a year, beginning a new
Thankful to God that He's brought us through.
We never know what a year will bring...
We trust the Lord for everything.

We're constantly yearning to hear God's voice
By His Holy Spirit, we'll make the right choice.
When skies are gray, no sun to see
We go to God's Word and find the key.

We don't find on earth our greatest treasure
It's the heavenly bank, no man can measure.
So stake your claim in this New Year...
He'll help you to keep it, without any fear.


For where your treasure is there will
your heart be also.


MATTHEW 6:21

# HOW WILL OTHERS SEE YOU

How will others see you
When you're dead and gone
Did they see you live for Jesus
Other's lives to spawn.

Did they see you love your spouse
More than you did yourself
Did they see you help your children
Or see you keep them on the shelf.

Did they see you lean on Jesus
For each and every need
Was your life like a Bible
That other's hearts could read.

You can't live for Jesus
No never on your own...
Trust in Jesus power
Interceding from God's throne.


Let no man despise your youth; but be thou
an example of the believers, in word, in
conversation, in charity, in spirit, in Faith,
in purity.

I TIMOTHY 4:12

# THE WAR

There's a war that's being fought
Each and every day.
It's not a war with tanks and guns
But one not far away.

It's not a war on foreign soil
It's fought on your domain,
And if you are not careful
Destruction will remain.

Be careful that the enemy
Doesn't come into your house.
He can easily get in by the way
You treat your spouse.

With computer and TV
Your enemy is free…
He's free to invade
If a watchman you won't be.

Give up selfishness and pride
Put them down on every side.
Put on God's armor everyday
You'll then be strong; He'll make a way.

If Jesus love flows in your home
The enemy won't want to roam.
Can't stand God's love and 'specially praise
So call in the army, their hands to raise.

Put on the whole armor of God that ye may
Be able to stand against the wiles
of the devil.

EPHESIANS 6:11

# THE WORKHOUSE

You've heard of different people
Who never can relax.
They always have to hurry
Just pushed to the max.

The place where they live
Is a workhouse, not a home.
The deer don't play
Nor buffalo roam.

There's discouraging words
And the skies are always cloudy.
Their home is a workhouse
No play, it's truly dowdy.

All work and no play
Makes Jack a dull boy.
Take time to play with children
To have some joy.

The times that kids remember
Were the wholesome games you played.
'Round the table face to face
And the times when you prayed.

When your family prays together
And they play together, too…
It's a very strong bond
That the devil can't break through.

He that loveth not knoweth not God;
for God is love.

I JOHN 4:8

Children's children are the crown of
old men; and the glory of children are their
fathers.
PROVERBS 17:6

# LIVE IN VICTORY

We want to be a winner
In this life we call a game.
Victory seems far off
On others try to blame.

We put the blame on others
Many times it's us
It only causes sorrow
To stir up such a fuss.

Knowing that sweet victory
Comes to the faithful few...
To those who seek God's kingdom first
Nothing else will do.

To many worldly others
It seems that you have lost,
But choosing God's kingdom
You've counted the cost.

You've counted the cost
The price you've paid...
No victory is sweeter
At His feet you've laid.

You've laid at His feet
Given God your heart,
Victory is sure
He'll do His part.

For whatsoever is born of God
overcometh the world: and this is the
victory that overcometh the world, even
our faith. Who is He that overcometh the
world, but he that believeth that Jesus is
the Son of God.

I JOHN 5:4, 5

# THE POTTER'S HAND

When God wants to use you
He brings out the wheel
God molds you with gentle hands
He knows how you feel.

Not one of us is like another
Your plan's different
Than sister and brother
With greater responsibility
You'll need more firing...
Wait and see.

We may not always understand
But we continue to hold God's hand.
When the process is complete...
Ministry's ready, stay at His feet.

Don't go farther than the Lord
Would ask.
He's made you ready, prepared
For the task.

The Lord is the potter
We are the clay—
He'll make you shine brighter
Like the Son's ray.

And the vessel that he made of clay was marred
in the hand of the potter: so he made it again another
vessel, as seemed good to the potter to make it.

JEREMIAH 18:4

# THE PENCIL

There is something that happens
When you pick up your pencil.
You may draw, write a list
Or trace through a stencil.

If you write a letter
To someone in need...
Your pencil writes words
From your soul, they might heed.

No one can write
Just like you do
What you feed in your mind
And your heart will come through.

Whatever you see
And read day by day...
Comes out through your pencil
When you write what you'd say.

Be careful to fill your heart, soul
And mind...
With God's wonderful Word
For the spiritually blind.

Finally, brethren, whatsoever things are true,
whatsoever things are just, whatsoever things are
pure, whatsoever things are lovely, whatsoever
things are of good report; if there be any virtue,
and if there be any praise, think on these things.

PHILIPIANS 4:8

# THE HURDLE

There's something you thought
You never could do...
The desire is lying
In the midst of the stew.

You see it's a hurdle
You can't run over...
Like the fear you had
When you played Red Rover.

The Lord wants to help you
Conquer this fear.
If He gives you desire
He'll make it clear.

He will clearly show
How the hurdle you can cross.
If you don't trust His guidance
It'll be your loss.

Don't wait another day
Get up, begin to run...
God's Word will give you courage
If your trust is in God's Son.


Commit thy way unto the Lord;
trust also in Him; and He shall bring
it to pass.

PSALM 37:5

# OUR PURPOSE

There's so much talk today
About having it all your way.
The world says look out for me
Find your purpose and you'll be free.

Everything centers around your dreams
Get what you want with worldly schemes
It's always about what I can do
Positive thinking won't get you through.

God's Word says seek Me first
Only that will quench your thirst.
If you always try to please yourself
Your heart will end up on a shelf.

Don't let self be your motivation
Spend time with God for revelation.
Let His plan be your purpose in life
It will be the end of all your strife.


If any man come after me, let him deny
himself, take up his cross, and follow me.

MATTHEW 16:24

# GOD'S LITTLE SURPRISES

We are creatures of habit
And like things to plan.
We have it down on paper
It's just a plan of man.

Then God sends a surprise
That's not in our order.
We wonder how it came
Right across the border.

It can be quite shocking
But surely as we know…
The Lord is working something
Just to help us grow.

Everything that happens
Even unsuspecting
He can use it for our good
If we're always connecting.


For we know that all things work
together for good to them who love God,
to them who are called according to His
purpose.

ROMANS 8:28

# A BALM THAT HEALS

Only the Lord can mend a heart
Because of the cross, He did His part.

He died on a cross to forgive our sin
All we should do is let Him in.

Let Jesus in to heal your pain
Then it will truly be heaven's gain.

His Spirit will comfort like no one else can
Surely the Lord has a heavenly plan.

God speaks through His Word that's sweeter than honey
It's a balm that heals, can't buy with money.


For God so loved the world, that He gave His only
begotten Son, that whosoever believeth in Him,
should not perish, but have everlasting life.

JOHN 3:16

But He was wounded for our transgressions,
He was bruised for our iniquities; the chastisement
of our peace was upon Him and with His stripes we are healed.

ISAIAH 53:5

# GREENER GRASS

If the grass is always greener on the other side of the fence
If we're always comparing, it don't make no sense.

Please excuse my English, it had to be said
The Lord is here to help us, no time for dread.

Dread about what someone might say about us
If we're not just like the Jones' oh what a fuss.

If we water and fertilize in God's Word every day
It will keep our grass green and we won't go astray.


But see ye first the kingdom of God and His righteousness,
and all these things shall be added
unto you.

MATTHEW 6:33

Take heed unto yourself and unto the Doctrine.
Continue in them, for in doing this you shall
both save yourself, and them who hear you.

I TIMOTHY 4:16

# HOPE

When life looks hopeless, so many things to do
Do not fear, do not doubt, I'll come through for you.

I am Your shield and buckler, I'll make My way so clear
Go to My Word and ask of Me, for I am very near.

If you never had to trust Me for big things in your life
You'd never grow in patience when life has dealt you strife.

Let my love continue, I'm as near as your last breath
I'll be there to comfort you until life ends in death.

Death is not the end you know, it's only the beginning
Because you have believed in Me, you will then be winning!


Now the God of hope fill you with all joy and peace
in believing, that ye may abound in hope, through
the power of the Holy Ghost.

ROMANS 15:13

# THAT PRECIOUS LINE

There's a highway of holiness
Where each of us must walk...
We've all heard the expression
We should walk our talk,

The only way that we can walk
That very precious line...
Is by trusting in our Savior
That awesome One so fine,

God will strengthen us and lead us
As we stay close to Him...
Then we'll not be deceived
By every new age whim

There's nothing more that we should do
He's paid the price for sin...
God sent Jesus to our world
Be sure to let Him in.


And an highway shall be there, and a way,
and it shall be called the way of holiness,
the unclean shall not pass over it; but it shall
be for those; the wayfaring men, though fools,
shall not err therein.

ISAIAH 35:8